The Magpie's Shadow

The Magpie's Shadow

Rcvd - Sept 1922

YVOR WINTERS

"No employment, my lor
A marginal note in the muster book, th
A voluntary lord."
                    —THE DUCHESS

The Magpie's Shadow

By

Yvor Winters

MUSTERBOOKHOUSE
CHICAGO
1922

To

M. V. C.

AND

H. B. S.

O saisons, ô châteaux!

I: In Winter

MYSELF

Pale mornings, and
I rise.

STILL MORNING

Snow air — my fingers curl.

AWAKENING

New snow, O pine of dawn!

WINTER ECHO

Thin air! My mind is gone.

THE HUNTER

Run! in the magpie's shadow.

NO BEING

I, bent. Thin nights receding.

II: IN SPRING

SPRING

I walk out the world's door.

MAY

Oh, evening in my hair!

SPRING RAIN

My doorframe smells of leaves.

SONG

Why should I stop for spring?

III: In Summer and Autumn

SUNRISE

Pale bees! — Oh, whither now?

FIELDS.

I did not pick
a flower.

AT EVENING

Like leaves my feet passed by.

COOL NIGHTS

At night bare feet on flowers!

SLEEP

Like winds my eyelids close.

THE ASPEN'S SONG

The summer holds me here.

THE WALKER

In dream, my feet are still.

BLUE MOUNTAIN

A deer walks that mountain.

GOD OF ROADS

I, peregrine of noon.

SEPTEMBER

Faint gold!   O think not here!

A DEER

The trees rose in the dawn.

MAN IN DESERT

His feet run as eyes blink.

DESERT

The tented autumn, gone!

THE END

Dawn rose, and desert shrunk.

MUSTERBOOK III

will contain the note-books of Szukalski with fourteen reproductions of his drawings. This book will be ready about April 1.

Other MUSTERBOOKS in preparation are:

POUL LUNOE: reproductions from the wood-cuts of this young Copenhagen artist.

UP MANY LADDERS: a lyric miscellany of poems, prose and drawings.

HERMAN SACHS: reproductions of his paintings, batiks designs and sketches.

EMANUEL CARNEVALI: poems and prose.

C. RAYMOND JONSON: reproductions of his paintings with a critical introduction.

ITALIAN POETRY: translations from the work of the younger Italian poets.

A few copies of MUSTERBOOK I. can still be had.

For further information, address:

MUSTERBOOKHOUSE

| Publication Office: | Editorial Office |
| 2103 North Halsted Street | 215 East Ontario Street |

CHICAGO

CPSIA information can be obtained
at www.ICGtesting.com
Printed in the USA
LVOW04s0741051017
551236LV00009B/11/P